A YEAR OF BLACK GIRL MAGIC

Pham, Kim. "Celebrating Black Joy as an Alternative Form of Resistance and Reclaiming of Humanity." Voice of OC, February 1, 2021. VoiceOfOC .org/2021/02/celebrating-black-joy-as-an-alternative-form-of -resistance-and-reclaiming-of-humanity.

"A Quote from Celebrations." Goodreads. Goodreads.com/quotes/115604 -let-gratitude-be-the-pillow-upon-which-you-kneel-to.

Vanzant, Iyanla. Quote Fancy. Quotefancy.com/quote/833683/Iyanla -Vanzant-We-think-we-have-to-do-something-to-be-grateful -or-something-has-to-be.

About the Author

From the time she was a girl, **Eboni Morgan**'s exploration of digital creation always centered on her experience as a young Black person. Through her online platform, Eboni Curls, she seeks to evoke healing, joy, and intentional self-love for Black women around the world. On her own self-love journey, she continues to grow, evolve, and share her experiences with her community in uplifting, inspirational media. Morgan is a proud sociology alumnus of Ryerson University and currently lives with her family and bunny, Nutmeg, in Ontario, Canada.

A YEAR OF
BLACK GIRL MAGIC

DAILY REFLECTIONS AND PRACTICES TO CELEBRATE BLACK WOMEN

EBONI MORGAN

ILLUSTRATION BY GRACE ENEMAKU

ROCKRIDGE
PRESS

Interior and Cover Designer: Angie Chu
Art Producer: Sara Feinstein
Editor: Crystal Nero
Production Editor: Dylan Julian
Production Manager: Sandy Noman

Illustration © 2021 Grace Enemaku. Author photo courtesy of Christine Cousins.

Paperback ISBN: 978-1-63807-044-3
eBook ISBN: 978-1-63807-155-6
R0

For my mother, Michelle;
my grandmother, Sweetie;
my granny, Gloria;
and my twin sister, Essence.
I am eternally grateful to you
for showing me real Black girl magic.

Contents

Introduction

The epitome of Black girl magic is who you are in this very moment. From the minute you pick up this book, you will embark on a journey that not only reminds you of your innate magic, but also encourages you to reignite it, hold it close, and cherish it for the rest of your life.

My name is Eboni Morgan and I am a digital content creator, writer, and model. I create content that celebrates and inspires Black women to lead an unapologetic life filled with self-love. As Black women, we often share discouraging and unsettling experiences around how we are treated, who we are told to be, and who we are *meant* to be. Mainstream media constantly paints negative images of us that don't embody who we truly are. Rarely are we able to create and share images from our own perspectives—images that show us to be the beautiful people we know and love. Time and time again, we are told that we are not valuable, not a priority, and not beautiful. We have been beaten down, held back, and gunned down by the systems that vow to protect us. In capturing and sharing the beauty I know exists in Black women, I've learned how important it is to quiet outside voices and to learn to bask in my Black girl magic with reverence.

CaShawn Thompson, the founder of the #BlackGirlMagic hashtag, took the hurtful, misogynistic, and racist words that are often hurled at Black women, and transformed them into something that embraces who we are at the core. She brought together a powerful community of Black women who understand the very magic we carry within us everywhere we go. Even when faced with hate, racism, sexism, and discrimination, Black women persevere. We thrive, we flourish, and we succeed. Our very existence is an ode to our magic—and we deserve to know and celebrate that as often as we can.

In my own journey to rediscovering my #BlackGirlMagic, I have unlearned and learned so much about unlocking the true magic within me. For many years, my self-esteem sank lower and lower, until it reached a dangerously low level I could no longer ignore. I was lost, depressed, unsure of who I was, and constantly bombarded with social media telling me I wasn't beautiful, valuable, or worthy. It was only through embarking on a personal journey of true self-love that I learned to acknowledge and embrace all that I am—and *that* is Black girl magic. Throughout this book, I will share the experiences, reflections, affirmations, practices, and words of encouragement that helped me get through the toughest of times in my own journey. I hope this book will be a helpful starting place for you to do the same. But if you are experiencing any ongoing or debilitating anxiety, depression, trauma, or fear, please reach out to a medical professional. This book is not a replacement for a therapist, medication, or medical treatment, and there is no shame in seeking professional help.

Although this path is a lifelong one, I hope my words will help spark your inner magic so you can continue on, knowing your true worth and beauty as a Black woman. I hope we can create an even stronger sisterhood of Black women who are aware of their bright light.

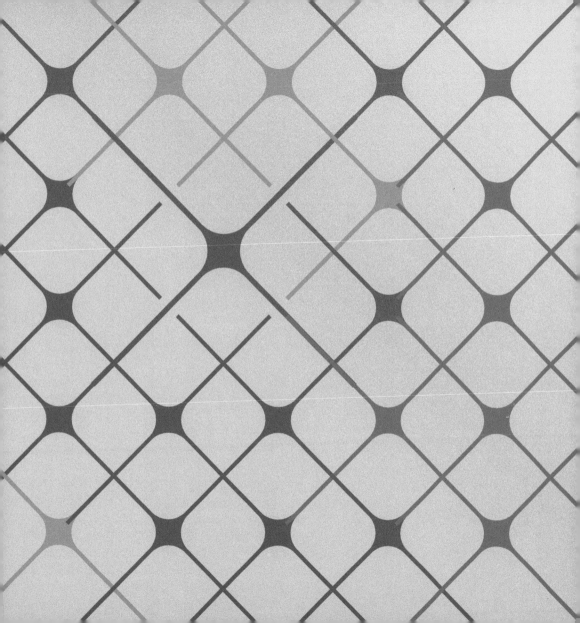

JANUARY
NEW
BEGINNINGS

1

JANURY

UNLOCKING YOUR MAGIC

As a Black woman, you've already got #BlackGirlMagic within you. It's in your smile and in your walk. It's your passion and the way you effortlessly break barriers. Look at yourself in the mirror and say, "I am filled with magic." Repeat it as many times as it takes for you to feel and believe the words coming out of your mouth (and do the same for the other affirmations sprinkled throughout this book).

In this journey, step one is simply acknowledging, honoring, and believing your own magic. Remember it every single day.

2

JANURY

When you commit to shifting your life in a positive direction, it will change. You must be willing to change with it in order to enjoy and experience this lifelong journey.

~~~

WELCOMING THE NEW YEAR

Allow yourself to welcome this year with open arms. Rather than focusing solely on the past, remember that you exist in the present. You cannot change the past and you cannot control the future—you can only exist in this very moment. Take some deep breaths, and then take a moment to focus on being present. What do you see or hear? How do you feel? What do you notice? You are here now and you have a brand-new opportunity to do whatever you'd like with each passing moment.

4

JANUARY

~~~

AFFIRMATION

I am worthy of my wildest dreams.

5

JANUARY

~~~

Although challenges can be frustrating and difficult,
they are vital to our personal growth.

Issa Rae is an American writer, actress, and producer. She began her career by creating a series called *Awkward Black Girl* on YouTube. Although Rae felt anxious and nervous about her career's humble beginnings, her creative work paid off and she became the producer of the extremely popular and successful HBO show *Insecure*. Had Rae given in to her fears of being different from her friends who pursued a more traditional route, she may have never reached the success she has today. Take a moment to think about simply starting something, no matter how impossible it may seem.

7

JANUARY

~

CELEBRATING YOUR WINS

Think back on the previous year. What are you proud of yourself for? What did you do that surprised you? What challenges did you overcome? What important lessons did you learn? Be proud of yourself for these wins, no matter how big or small. When we take the time to celebrate ourselves, we learn to accept and embrace who we are in the present moment.

8

JANUARY

~

Show up as the woman you hope to be someday, every day.

9

JANUARY

~~~

BE GRATEFUL FOR GROWTH

As we continue to grow every day, it's important to reflect on our journey and to be grateful for our beautiful growth. Take some time to reflect on your childhood self. Would she be proud of who you have become today? You wouldn't be who you are now if you weren't who you were in your past. Be grateful for your journey and growth—it's uniquely yours and beautiful in its own way.

10

JANUARY

~~~

Set goals that push you to become a better version of yourself over and over again. There is no finish line, just the opportunity to choose to be better each and every day.

11
JANUARY

~

DREAM BIGGER

Carve out some time to make a list of the goals you would like to accomplish. These goals can be specific to what you want to accomplish this year, or beyond—there is no specific time line. Remember you are allowed to dream as big as you can imagine. It's important to focus on your dreams, so try not to let yourself fall into limiting thoughts or beliefs. You are truly capable of *anything* you put your mind to—trust and believe it! Be sure to write down at least five goals that scare you.

12
JANUARY

~

What you think and what you believe are both true.

13

JANUARY

ALIGNING WITH YOUR GOALS

Think about a time when you had a big job interview or had to try out for a team. You had to show that you were the perfect fit for the role before actually attaining it. It's the same when it comes to setting goals. Show yourself and the Universe that you're capable of achieving these goals by playing the role of someone who has already achieved them. Think about what your life would be like right now if you had already achieved every goal on the list you created. What can you do now to align with those goals?

14

JANUARY

Your best is enough.

15
JANUARY

EMBRACING CHALLENGES

Challenges cannot be avoided in any journey. No matter what you do, you will encounter a challenge at some point. Instead of looking at challenges as negatives, think of them as steps toward becoming a stronger, better version of yourself. If you hadn't overcome challenges on your journey, you wouldn't be where you are right now. Think about someone you admire and everything they've accomplished. What challenges do you think they had to overcome to be the inspirational person they are to you now?

16
JANUARY

"Taking up space" requires us to give ourselves permission to truly exist. Rather than making yourself smaller to fit in somewhere, analyze the space and allow yourself to simply be there. Remember that you deserve to be in that space.

17
JANUARY

MAINTAINING A POSITIVE MINDSET

Ever notice that when you're having a bad day, everything just seems to go wrong? This is a perfect example of how we manifest our thoughts. The more thoughts we give our precious energy to, the faster our reality will manifest these thoughts. Each time you talk to yourself throughout the day, be mindful of what you're saying and how you're saying it. It's important to find a balance between being honest and realistic with yourself, and speaking to yourself with love and respect. The goal is to build a space in your mind that's healthy to be in.

18

JANUARY

When we step back from trying to control time,
we give ourselves the opportunity to enjoy it.

19

JANUARY

CLEANSING YOUR SPACE

Often, especially as Black women, we are expected to make ourselves smaller to "fit in" to other spaces. Keeping our homes and workspaces free of mess allows us to exist comfortably and openly and reminds us that we are worthy of taking up space and deserve to live in cleanliness—both physically and mentally. It also means cleansing your space of negative energies. Think back to a time you felt comfortable and safe, knowing you were in a clean space. What did it feel like? Smell like? Look like?

20
JANUARY

If you take just one step toward your goals every day,
you'll find them much more attainable than trying
to achieve them all at once.

21
JANUARY

AFFIRMATION

My mind is a safe and welcoming space.

22

JANUARY

TRUST THAT TIME IS IN YOUR FAVOR

Sometimes when things don't go our way, we get frustrated and scared that things are "running off track." We begin to feel anxious and annoyed, and we forget that things take time. My grandma always tells me that anything worth having will take time. Each step you take is just another stepping-stone on your journey. Think about a time when things went differently than you originally planned, but in the end it worked out to your benefit. Cherish the time you have now and remember to enjoy the process.

23

JANUARY

~~~

If one has courage, nothing can dim the light that shines from within.

—DR. MAYA ANGELOU

24

JANUARY

~~~

Unlocking your Black girl magic means committing to delving deep within yourself. It means getting to know who you are at the core and embracing every single bit of it.

25

JANUARY

〜

TRY YOUR BEST

We cannot be perfect at everything. Very often, we habitually punish ourselves for not doing a "better" job. Recognize that your best will look different every day, but it is truly all you can ask of yourself. Be honest with yourself and respect your efforts. Today and each day following, make a promise to yourself that you will do your best, however that may look to you.

26

JANUARY

〜

Reflect on the previous year. Think back to your accomplishments and intentionally celebrate them. Remind yourself that you made it through some of the toughest days—that is worth celebrating!

27
JANUARY

~

A LITTLE EACH DAY GOES A LONG WAY

On this journey, there will be times when you feel overwhelmed, but remember that you don't need to accomplish everything at once. In the race between the turtle and the hare, you are the turtle. Taking one or a few steps every day will get you to the finish line with more knowledge and a deeper understanding of your own magic. Using the list of goals you created on January 11, write down one step you can take today toward achieving one goal. We all have to start somewhere!

28
JANUARY

~

Be grateful for the woman you once were. You had to walk in her shoes to become the woman you are today.

29
JANUARY

~

Naomi Campbell is a famous British supermodel and fashion icon, largely known for her beautiful dark complexion and killer runway walk. As a Black model, Campbell regularly faced racism and discrimination. Today, as an advocate for Black models, Campbell has created a number of opportunities for aspiring Black models and Black women worldwide. She says, "Am I bossy? Absolutely. I don't like to lose, and if I'm told no, then I find another way to get my yes. But I'm a loyal person." Take a moment to think about how Campbell has used being told no as fuel for her success.

30
JANUARY

~~~

What you know today can affect what you do tomorrow. But what you know today cannot affect what you did yesterday.

—CONDOLEEZZA RICE

31
JANUARY

~~~

AFFIRMATION

I actively make space for fresh, new,
and abundant energy in my life.

FEBRUARY
SELF-LOVE

1

FEBRUARY

~~~

REFLECTION TIME

Take some time to reflect on what January was like for you. When we begin a new month, it's important to get into the habit of pausing, looking back, and taking time to prepare for the month ahead. It's also a healthy way to hold yourself accountable for your own goals and aspirations. Here are some questions to ask yourself: What am I proud of myself for from the last month? What can I improve? What do I need more of this month?

2

FEBRUARY

~~~

When we give ourselves time to reflect along our journey, we gift ourselves the chance to move forward with our inner wisdom.

3

FEBRUARY

WHAT DOES YOUR OWN COMPANY FEEL LIKE?

Think back to the last time you thoroughly enjoyed your own presence. Did you dance around, carefree? Did you let yourself laugh uncontrollably? Did you sit in peace or enjoy a quiet morning to yourself? If you can't think back to a time you experienced this, imagine what it feels like to truly enjoy being in your own company.

SPEAK TO YOURSELF

Find a mirror, take a few deep breaths, and then look directly at your reflection. Now tell yourself 10 different things you love about yourself. They can be character traits, body parts, beauty marks—absolutely anything you like about yourself. No matter how small it is or how tough this may be, make sure you intentionally say and mean 10 different things. Use your own voice to shower yourself with positivity!

5
FEBRUARY

~~~

Self-love is less about what it looks like,
and more about what it feels like.

6
FEBRUARY

~~~

There is so much power in the words we say.
We can bring that power to life simply by speaking
positively every day.

7

FEBRUARY

~~~

Serena Williams is a wildly talented, world-renowned tennis champion. Despite her countless wins, she has faced many disparaging comments about her demeanor and her body, some of which compare her physique to that of a man. Williams has continued to dominate in her sport, in addition to launching her own venture capital firm and clothing line. Take some time to contemplate Serena's unapologetic love for tennis and her body, and how it allowed her to become one of the best athletes in the world.

8

FEBRUARY

~~~

SPEAK TO YOURSELF WITH RESPECT

Throughout today, be very mindful of how you speak to yourself both aloud and in your mind. Always remember that you breathe life into the words you speak internally and externally. When you are mean to yourself, you trick yourself into believing that the horrible things you say are true. The longer you maintain this mindset, the harder it gets to pull yourself out of it. When you live in positivity, you radiate it both inward and outward.

9

FEBRUARY

When we learn to love ourselves unconditionally, we can share that same love with our friends, family, loved ones, and community. Choosing to love ourselves is also choosing to love the people around us.

10
FEBRUARY

~~~

HAVE A CONVERSATION WITH YOURSELF

Set aside some time to find a quiet space and have a conversation with yourself, out loud. Tell yourself about your day, what you enjoyed, and what you noticed. When we learn to have conscious, vulnerable conversations with ourselves, we build a healthy ability to trust our instincts and intuition. It might feel weird to say these things out loud, but remember that you have simple conversations with people almost every day. You are more than capable of talking to yourself!

11
FEBRUARY

How we speak to ourselves is everything. Whether we think we are capable or not, intelligent or not, successful or not—we are correct. It is important to remember to speak to ourselves with the utmost respect.

12
FEBRUARY

WHO ARE YOU?

As Black women, we are constantly told who we are "meant" to be from the time we are children. Many of us grew up understanding ourselves through the images we were fed and continue to be fed in the media. Before we can figure out who we are, what we like, or what we dislike, it is predetermined—but it's often incorrect and detrimental to who we truly are. Take some time to reflect on some traits or actions you may have internalized as a young Black girl or as a Black woman because you thought you had to.

13
FEBRUARY

Showering ourselves with intentional love disrupts
harmful, hurtful, and racist Eurocentric beauty
standards that have been placed on us.
It also encourages our sisters to celebrate
and love themselves.

14
FEBRUARY

HOW DO YOU LOVE YOUR BODY?

What's your favorite way to show your body you love it? I love taking
time to dress up my body and celebrate every roll and every flaw, just
the way it is. If you aren't sure, try asking yourself these questions to
get started: What makes my body feel good? What reminds me of the
love I have for my body? How can I show my body how much I love it?

Each time you compare yourself to someone else,
you rob yourself of the joy that comes with your
own beautiful, individual journey.

16
FEBRUARY

YOU ARE BEAUTIFUL

Although many of us are finally learning our beauty, Black women continue to battle the beauty industry. For many years, we have been told that our complexions, lips, hair, and bodies are ugly, while the bodies and faces of lighter-skinned people are celebrated. But even though our features may not be openly celebrated online or in the media, we have the power to celebrate and love ourselves as a radical act against Eurocentric beauty standards. Celebrate the things you were told aren't beautiful! The more we embrace who we are, the more we can grow in self-love.

17
FEBRUARY

Loving yourself is a nonlinear process. But remember you have a new opportunity to choose to love yourself with each and every moment.

18
FEBRUARY

~~~

If we give our children sound self-love, they will be able to deal with whatever life puts before them.

—BELL HOOKS

19
FEBRUARY

~~~

BE PROUD OF YOURSELF

Throughout this journey, it can be challenging to keep track of and celebrate our wins in a productive way. Celebrating yourself is just one way to show yourself love. Write a list of all the things you are proud of accomplishing, no matter how big or small. Make the list as long as possible and remind yourself you did all that! Spend some time in that congratulatory space.

20
FEBRUARY

Be consistent and intentional in the love you show yourself.

21
FEBRUARY

AFFIRMATION

I love and accept myself exactly where
I am at this moment.

22
FEBRUARY

~

CELEBRATE YOUR SUPPORTERS

Write down a list of all the people who openly support and love you. When times get tough—and they will—it's important to have a group of people who love you and bring out the best in you. They can be family, friends, or loved ones—reliable people you can call on and who genuinely want the best for you. Once you identify these people, take some time to call them or send them a thoughtful message. Remember that healing is embedded in the community and the company we keep.

23
FEBRUARY

~

Unlearn who you have been told to be and embrace who you are.

REMEMBER WHO YOU ARE

Black History Month is a time to reflect and gather energy, love, and wisdom from our ancestors and communities. In school, we are briefly taught that Black history simply begins and ends with slavery. Black people were not slaves, but intelligent, beautiful, valuable, and loved people who were enslaved for generations. Take some time to reflect on the resilience and strength of our people. Think about who we were and who we are, compared with how we are portrayed.

25
FEBRUARY

~~~

Building a circle of people who truly love and admire you
is part of a successful self-love journey.

26
FEBRUARY

~~~

AFFIRMATION

I am deserving of unconditional love.

27
FEBRUARY

~~~

Michelle Obama, American attorney and former First Lady of the United States, has faced countless disparaging remarks about her appearance and success. Think about what her journey might have looked like if she had not built a strong foundation of self-love.

28
FEBRUARY

~~~

When we revel in the abundant beauty of our people, our ancestors, and our cultures, we build our ability to see that same beauty in ourselves. Celebrate your Blackness every chance you get!

29

FEBRUARY

I don't have any time to stay up all night worrying about what someone who doesn't love me has to say about me.

—VIOLA DAVIS

MARCH
SELF-CARE

1

MARCH

~~

EXPLORE MOTHER NATURE

Take some time to head outdoors and enjoy the fresh air. Give yourself space to exist and explore. Enjoying Mother Nature and her beautiful gifts allows us to ground and reconnect with our true selves.

2

MARCH

~~

Self-care looks different for everybody. We all have different needs, wants, and desires. The common denominator in all our journeys is that we deserve to grow and find what feels good to us.

3

MARCH

~~~

HAVE FUN!

Think of a fun activity you enjoyed as a child. During the next week, schedule some time to revisit this activity. Remember that you deserve to have fun. Allow yourself to enjoy the experience—you might just pick up this hobby again!

4

MARCH

A balanced diet includes more than what you eat or drink. It also encompasses what you are watching, what you are listening to, who you are around, and the type of conversations you entertain.

5

MARCH

EVALUATE YOUR SOCIAL MEDIA

If you use social media, take some time to review your feed on different apps. Pay close attention to how you feel after scrolling. Is what you are seeing exciting or fulfilling? Or does it leave you feeling drained, tired, or self-critical? If it's the latter, take some time to clean up who you're following and filter what you're seeing. A healthy social media feed should leave you feeling inspired, strong, and capable.

6

MARCH

No self-care ritual is static. Each day, we may be pulled to do something a little differently than the day before. Give yourself space to explore and find new ways to care for and love yourself.

7

MARCH

〜〜

Intersectionality describes the intersection of racism and sexism that Black women experience. The intersections can even multiply, based on sexual preference, complexion, social class, and so on. The term was coined by Kimberlé Williams Crenshaw, an American lawyer, philosopher, and civil rights advocate who explored how this type of oppression creates a uniquely challenging experience for Black women. In reflecting on intersectionality, think about the Black woman's experience, and what self-care for us looks like compared with others who do not face the challenges we do each day.

MARCH

CREATE PEACEFUL MORNINGS

For the next week, spend at least 15 minutes alone in the morning before starting your day. Taking this time before tackling your to-do list can do so much for boosting your mental wellness and setting a calm, pleasurable tone for the day. Even if the day doesn't go as planned, you can continue on, knowing you intentionally filled your cup. As you grow on this journey, you can expand this time to 30 minutes or even an hour. Try not to spend any of this time scrolling on your phone or distracting yourself in other ways.

MARCH

The care we wished for as children is the same care we need as we grow up. Care for yourself as though you were your childhood self.

10

MARCH

SHOW YOURSELF LOVE THROUGH FOOD

It can be very challenging to motivate yourself to cook for just one person. It was a huge struggle for me, until I learned that cooking for myself is an act of self-care, not just a task or a chore. When was the last time you cooked a delicious, nourishing meal for yourself? Take some time to find an exciting recipe to make. You are deserving of a filling meal that nourishes your beautiful body!

11

MARCH

Self-care is not selfish.

12
MARCH

~

AFFIRMATION

I take care of myself because I love myself.

13
MARCH

~

PARENT YOURSELF

We often fault our parents for not giving us the care we felt we needed as children. As we grow, it becomes our own responsibility to care for ourselves in the ways we needed. Take some time to think back to your childhood and the type of care you wanted. Instead of getting angry, give yourself that exact same care. If you wanted more quality time, spend some time with yourself. If you needed more physical touch, move your body or massage yourself. You deserve to be cared for in a way that makes you feel happy and secure!

14
MARCH

When we intentionally love ourselves, self-care becomes
an extension of the love we have for ourselves.

15
MARCH

TRY JOURNALING

Caring for our mental well-being can set the tone for how we lead our
lives each day. When our minds are full and we are busy, our self-care
needs sometimes fall to the back burner. To manage your thoughts
and emotions, try journaling. There is no word count requirement, no
rules—you can write as little or as much as you like. The goal is to give
your mind a rest by getting your thoughts and emotions on paper. It is
also a great way to dig deep to find out how you're truly feeling.

16

MARCH

~~~

You must care for yourself before you can care for others.

17

MARCH

~~~

Ericka Huggins is an American civil rights activist and former leader of the Black Panther Party. While she was incarcerated, Huggins turned to meditation to build and maintain a healthy state of mind. She continued to practice it throughout her life after being released from prison, and now promotes it as a means of retaliation against white supremacy in America. Think about what a powerful tool meditation can be when you're facing such challenges and opposition.

18

MARCH

LOVE OTHERS BY LOVING YOURSELF

Although self-care begins with the self, it also includes our relationships and how we are around others. Sometimes caring for yourself means saying no to things you don't want or exercising your boundaries. It may come across as selfish to many people, but remember that by choosing to care for yourself you are choosing to care for others. Before you say yes to the next outing, party, or favor for someone else, ask yourself: Will I feel better or worse afterward? Does where I'm heading make me feel safe? Would this person do the same for me?

19

MARCH

Nourishing the body takes many forms. Rest, food, joy, and love are just a few ways to introduce yourself to lifelong nourishment.

20

~

Caring for myself is not self-indulgence, it is self-preservation, and that is an act of political warfare.

—AUDRE LORDE

21
MARCH

~

SELF-CARE IS A JOURNEY

We often look at self-care as a means to an end. When we are tired, restless, or sad, we treat these feelings as cues that self-care can simply "fix." But it's actually the opposite—we need to practice some form of self-care every day to maintain a healthy, balanced lifestyle. Starting today, try to incorporate some type of self-care into your day, whether it be mental, physical, or social. Staying consistent on this journey will help you reap lasting benefits.

22
MARCH

~~~

In the media, we see self-care portrayed as a hot bubble bath, a fancy spa treatment, and a day off. But much of your self-care journey will take place mentally, and will likely require a lot of challenges, unlearning, and relearning. Be open to and accepting of this new journey!

23

MARCH

~~~

PRACTICE, PRACTICE, PRACTICE

Sometimes we get wrapped up in self-care as an act rather than a practice. The more we practice self-care, the more we strengthen our sense of what we need. Make a list of five things you need from yourself right now. It may be a break from hard work, some fresh air, or time to meditate. No matter what it is, be sure to make it a consistent practice to check in with yourself.

24

MARCH

~~~

Many of us mistake surviving for living. When we constantly operate in survival mode, we lose sight of the abundant beings we are. Through intentionally caring for ourselves, we can learn to live, and even flourish, instead of always just surviving through life.

25

MARCH

~~~

AFFIRMATION

I deserve to be cared for with love.

26

MARCH

~~~

QUALITY, NOT QUANTITY

Sometimes the smallest acts of self-care carry us the furthest. Now that you know self-care doesn't have to be extravagant, think of just one small new way you can take better care of yourself. It could be waking up earlier so you have more time to yourself before work, doing more physical activity throughout the week, or meditating to clear your mind before you go to sleep.

27
MARCH

~~~

Some days may require more self-care than others. It's important to listen to the messages your mind, body, and spirit are communicating to you. Only when you stop and listen can you determine your best next steps.

28
MARCH

~~~

TRUST YOURSELF

On this journey, old beliefs will attempt to sway your path. You might begin to think you're undeserving of this new care or feel tempted to jump back into your old ways. Each time one of these negative thoughts comes up, imagine yourself writing it down on a piece of paper and tearing it up. Better yet, make an actual list of all your fears, doubts, and conflicts about caring for yourself and tear it up. Remind yourself that your journey is yours, and you are allowed to grow and change into a better version of yourself through self-care.

29
MARCH

Allowing yourself some quiet time and space before you start your day is one way to reclaim your time.

30
MARCH

Stop allowing the past to anchor your future.

We have so much coming in as sisters. When is our interior life ever put at the forefront? We constantly want to give to other people. The word *no* is important. It's self-abuse. Too much of not caring for yourself is not a good thing. We're bad at that as achievers. Self-care is a priority, and we have to do it more.

—AVA DUVERNAY

APRIL
REFRESH

APRIL

SIMPLICITY IS KEY

Think about how refreshing a cool drink of water is on a hot summer day or how a comforting bowl of soup feels on a cold or rainy day. Reflect on how something so simple can revitalize and replenish your spirit.

APRIL

Spring always brings a refreshed feeling following the winter months. Just like the seasons, life is a cycle of dormancy—sometimes death and sometimes rebirth.

3

APRIL

ENJOY MOTHER NATURE

Take some time to get out and enjoy this shift in nature. Even if you live in a place where the climate is mostly the same year-round, you can learn so much about your own life cycles by being in nature and enjoying the gifts it offers in different seasons. You just might see something you've never noticed before!

4

APRIL

We have the opportunity to revive ourselves every day by completing small actions that replenish us.

5
APRIL

APRIL SHOWERS BRING MAY FLOWERS

There's a saying that goes: "April showers bring May flowers." Without the support of the rain, crops wouldn't grow and flowers wouldn't bloom. Reflect on how important it is to nourish and care for yourself so you can continue being the best version of yourself.

6
APRIL

It can be particularly challenging to reinvigorate our lives when we continue the same cycle day after day. To grow, we must try new things, challenge ourselves, and get familiar with failing.

APRIL

~~~

WHAT DOES YOUR BODY NEED?

Following a time of heavy emotional lifting and growth, rest is necessary to replenish yourself. Reflect on the last time you woke up feeling refreshed from a nap or a deep sleep. What does this tell you about what you and your body need to be your best self?

APRIL

~~~

When we open ourselves up to new and different experiences, we allow ourselves to enjoy life on a grander, more enjoyable scale.

9

APER

Candis Peniston is an Afro-Caribbean-Canadian registered social worker, psychotherapist, and spiritual director. Through counseling, Peniston focuses largely on dismantling stigmas around mental health issues in Black and racialized communities. Peniston's framework is centered around healing in an African cultural context. Think about how refreshing it can feel to open up to someone who seeks to help and understand you on a deeper, more interconnected level.

10

APRIL

WHAT ARE YOUR SOCIAL MEDIA HABITS?

Social media has largely impacted our ability to experience and share new things without an audience, "likes," or "views" attached to it. This month, reflect on the amount of time you spend on your smartphone and/or on social media. Try limiting your screen time to a span that is comfortable to you. This will allow you to spend less time online and more time truly enjoying your life.

11
APART APRIL

Technology has commanded the attention of humans
on a worldwide scale. People spend more and
more time than ever online, absorbing information,
notifications, and content. We spend countless hours
"refreshing" our feeds, but how much time do we
dedicate to "refreshing" ourselves?

12

APPL

CHECK YOUR ACCESSIBILITY

Being completely accessible at all times through our cell phones has become a social norm. It often limits our ability to focus on our tasks and our day-to-day lives without interruption. Try turning off your phone notifications for at least 30 minutes each day. You'll be surprised at how refreshing it may feel to answer a text when you get to it, rather than immediately after receiving it.

13
APRIL

〰

I love myself when I am laughing . . . and then again when I am looking mean and impressive.

—ZORA NEALE HURSTON

14
APRIL

〰

AFFIRMATION

I let go of that which no longer serves me.

15
APRIL

SLOW DOWN WHEN YOU CAN'T STOP

Sometimes when we need a rest, we are still in a time of action. Life is still happening and we simply don't have the time to stop. Although now may not necessarily be a time for rest, what small things can you do to help keep yourself energized each day? Think about what foods or activities refresh you. You may just find a new way to motivate yourself to keep going!

16
APRIL

When we get rid of things that no longer serve us, we show the Universe that we are actively creating the space to accept new blessings.

17
APRIL

~~

REFRESH AT HOME

Envision your dream vacation destination. How would it replenish you? How would it feel to return to your life after this vacation? What activities would you try? Once you're finished, reflect on these things. Choose one you can do to refresh yourself right now, where you are.

18
APPRIL

Acknowledging—and then removing—the thoughts and emotions we've swept under the rug helps us feel light and refreshed.

19
APPRIL

SPRING CLEAN YOUR SPACE

Carve out some time for a little spring cleaning over the course of this week. Choose a small space to start without pressuring yourself to accomplish everything at once. When we give ourselves time to work through our cleaning, it allows us to see the benefit of committing to creating a cleaner space to live in. We see the gradual changes and can enjoy our spaces when we finish, knowing we've done something to support a healthier lifestyle.

20

APRIL

~~~

**Instead of looking at the past,
I put myself ahead 20 years and
try to look at what I need to do now
in order to get there then.**

—DIANA ROSS

21
APRIL

～

Engaging in stimulating conversations is just
a simple way to allow others to pour into us through
their words and wisdom.

22
APRIL

～

REFRESH YOUR DIET

During the spring, I like to take time to cleanse my body to get back to
feeling my healthiest. Sometimes our diet can make it difficult for our
body to continue digesting and operating at its best. We can give it a
break by eating foods that sustain and nourish us. Nurture your body
by consuming more water, raw fruits, and fresh vegetables. Try finding
a recipe with fruits and vegetables that excites you!

23
APRIL

~~~

Much like spring cleaning, now is an optimal time
to declutter your spirit.

24
APRIL

~~~

CHAT WITH YOUR LOVED ONES

In February, you created a list of friends, family, and loved ones who
genuinely support you. This week, choose three people from that list
to connect with. If you can, try to call or meet with them just to have
a conversation. It can be about anything that brings you both some
joy. Maintaining healthy relationships with important people can be
extremely rejuvenating.

25
APRIL

Allow yourself to sow seeds of abundance during this lush season. If you want to see the results later, start now.

26
APRIL

MEET SOMEONE NEW

Challenge yourself to meet someone new this week. As we change and interact with new people, they can teach us so much on this path of growth. It can be so refreshing to meet someone with a new perspective and a different understanding of the world than ours. These energizing interactions also push us to live fuller, more dimensional lives!

27

APRIL

~~~

Clear your space of any excess. When we carry too much, it weighs us down and holds us back from receiving our rightful gifts.

28
APRIL

~~~

Jodianne Beckford, a Canadian-Caribbean photographer and the founder of the plant group Noire Girls Plant, facilitates hikes and creates spaces for Black women to bond, heal, and learn through nature. Not only do these hikes encourage interaction and love through sisterhood, they also allow hikers to embrace the outdoors in a welcoming, enjoyable way. Reflect on how refreshing it can be to reconnect with Mother Earth through community, the way our ancestors did.

29
APRIL

~~~

AFFIRMATION

I allow myself to experience and enjoy new things.

30

Sometimes you've got to let everything go—purge yourself. If you are unhappy with anything . . . whatever is bringing you down, get rid of it. Because you'll find that when you're free, your true creativity, your true self comes out.

—TINA TURNER

MAY
BEING
PRESENT

1

MAY

ACCEPT YOUR PRESENT SELF

Take some time to focus on where you are in your journey at this present moment. Try not to get distracted by who you want to become and avoid judging yourself. Practice accepting yourself in this very moment.

2

MAY

Appreciate every moment of your individual journey. It's all yours.

3

MAY

GROUND YOURSELF

When we become overwhelmed with the number of things we must do, it can be difficult to remain present. Before tackling anything on your list, try grounding yourself by taking a few long, deep breaths. Let yourself simply exist and be aware of the present.

4

MAY

You are exactly where you're supposed to be.

5

MAY

MAGNIFY YOUR GRATITUDE

Make a list of everything you are grateful for at this exact time. When we can home in on what we're grateful for, we remind ourselves of the goodness and blessings we experience each and every day.

6

MAY

When we focus on our endless to-do lists,
we forget to cherish the moments we have outside
of completing these tasks.

7
MAY

TUNE IN

Tune in to your surroundings. What do you see? What does it smell like? What do you hear? Allow your body to communicate with you through your senses.

8
MAY

A large part of being present is trusting yourself. Trust that you are doing your best, and that will inevitably set you up for success in the future.

9
MAY

PRACTICE JOURNALING

One way I've strengthened my ability to be present is through journaling. It allows me to get my thoughts sorted on paper instead of jumbled in my mind. Make some time to create your own journal if you don't have one. Each day, write at least one sentence about anything at all. You'll find that it pulls you into your experience in the exact moment you are writing.

10
MAY

Remember that you are constantly growing and evolving. Although you may not be able to achieve something at this stage in your journey, have faith in your ability to become someone who is able to accomplish that same goal in the future.

11
MAY

AFFIRMATION

I accept and love myself entirely.

12
MAY

UPDATE YOUR ACCOMPLISHMENTS

Sometimes it can be challenging to see our own growth and the person we have become without some reflection. Spend some time listing your accomplishments. As we've begun the second quarter of the year, updating your list along the way may help you see and accept how much you've done.

13
MAY

Be intentional in how you engage in conversation. Our minds often wander or we may talk over people when we have conversations. By being present, we can engage in more insightful, fulfilling conversations with our loved ones.

14

MAY

Tracee Ellis Ross is an American actress, singer, producer, and director. In an interview with Oprah Winfrey, Ellis Ross discussed learning to view the present as a gift. Through living life slowly and fully, Ellis Ross credits being present for reminding her to take her time caring for herself and truly enjoying life. She uses soup as an example of being present. A hot bowl of soup cannot be eaten quickly. It requires you to sit and truly be present with each spoonful. In thinking about this analogy, reflect on how simple the practice of being present can be.

15
MAY

LAY YOUR ANXIETIES TO REST

Reflect on the last time you were present enough to lay your anxieties about the future and regrets about the past to rest. Did you feel carefree? What did you spend this time doing? If you can't think back to a time you felt present, imagine what it would feel like to simply focus on enjoying the present moment.

16
MAY

Do not rush divine timing.

17
MAY

DO NOT DISTURB

Day-to-day life is filled with many different interruptions. One of the most common interruptions are the notifications we receive on our phones. When we are constantly choosing these interruptions instead of being in the present, it can strengthen the hold that anxiety and depression often have on us. When you are trying to be present, try putting your phone on silent, or, better yet, somewhere out of reach. It will be challenging, but you'll be grateful for the times you spent looking up instead of down.

18
MAY

Although it's extremely helpful to dream and imagine what the future will be like, it's equally important to be grateful for where you are in this exact moment. Showing gratitude is one of the best ways to accept where we are on this journey.

19
MAY

～

TAKE TIME WITH YOUR TASKS

With each task you complete today, no matter how big or small, try to be present. The more you practice being present, the easier it becomes to remind yourself to remain present in challenging times.

20
MAY

～

Breathe. Let go. And remind yourself that this very moment is the only one you know you have for sure.

—OPRAH WINFREY

21

MAY

~~~~~

SPEND YOUR TIME WISELY

When we focus on the past, we lose sight of the present and often torture ourselves, wishing things went differently. Reflect on a time when you were so worried over something in the past that you couldn't stop thinking about it. Did thinking about it alter the outcome? Did it make you feel better or worse?

22
MAY

~~~~~

There are two things you have control over in this lifetime: yourself and the present.

23
MAY

~~~

BEING VERSUS DOING

Sometimes being present looks like spending time *being* rather than *doing*. It can be a very challenging thing to practice, especially if you are used to constantly working or are not familiar with calming the mind. Tonight before you go to sleep, try to spend some time being instead of doing anything. Being still allows you to relish the present, unconcerned by any upcoming tasks or chores.

24
MAY

~~~

Regardless of how your day has gone up to this point,
remember you are here in the present with no control
of the past. Allow yourself the peace of moving forward,
creating the rest of your day however you wish.

25
MAY

~~~

AFFIRMATION

I trust that divine timing always works in my favor.

26
MAY

~

YOU ARE WHERE YOU ARE MEANT TO BE

Where you are in this very moment is exactly where you're meant to be. Whenever you feel you should be further ahead or that you should've accomplished more, remind yourself that you're exactly where you're meant to be. As clichéd as it may sound, patience is a virtue and very necessary for your well-being!

27
MAY

~

Your to-do list can wait. Be present through laughter,
spend time with the ones you love,
and enjoy your life right now.

28
MAD
MAY

FOCUS ON THE JOURNEY

Be patient on this journey. Each time you find yourself getting frustrated that you aren't further ahead, remember that the Egyptian pyramids weren't built in a day. It takes time, growth, and a lot of patience. This path is about the journey, not the destination.

29
MAY

Let go of who people tell you to be
and start embracing who you are.

30
MAY

Dr. Crystal Jones is a presence coach, dynamic anchor, and sound therapist. Through her work, Dr. Jones uses sound to help clients anchor themselves in the present moment, instead of being stuck in the past or anxious about the future. With intentional sound, prayer, and silence, Dr. Jones has helped many women learn to embed themselves in the present moment without fear. Take a moment to think about the many different ways you can practice being present.

31
MAY

~~~

Every great dream begins with a dreamer. Always remember, you have within you the strength, the patience, and the passion to reach for the stars to change the world.

—HARRIET TUBMAN

JUNE
JOY

~~~

YOUR JOY IS A PRIORITY

We often let our busy lives get in the way of prioritizing our own happiness. We fall into the habit of making joy a reward for our hard work, instead of something we should experience for its own sake. To combat this, it's important to learn that you don't have to accomplish anything to experience joy. Today, try to find joyful ways to cross off everything on your to-do list. Be creative!

2

JUNE

~~~

To wait for bad things to happen is to rob yourself of joy.

3
JUNE

WHAT DOES YOUR JOY LOOK LIKE?

Reflect on the last time you experienced true, raw, authentic joy. What did it look like? What did it feel like? How did you embrace your own joy? If you can't think of the last time you experienced joy, think of what brings you joy and happiness.

4
JUNE

You are worthy of joy.

5
JUNE

Esther Fagbamila is a cofounder of Upset Homegirls, a nonprofit organization that promotes social justice and opposes systemic racism. Fagbamila contends that "Black Joy" has a place everywhere, especially during protests. Rather than ask attendees to chant or bring signs, Upset Homegirls encourages attendees to dance. Think about how you can use joy to serve more than just happiness.

JUNE

~

EVALUATE WHAT BRINGS YOU JOY

We're often told that we need material items—shoes, bags, cars, clothes, etc.—to experience joy. We have all experienced joy relating to material things, but it's important not to make them our only source of joy. Today, think about your belongings. What do you own that brings you joy? What brought you joy in the past? If something doesn't bring you happiness now, evaluate whether it's a necessity.

JUNE

~

Cherish those whose joy is also your joy.

JUNE

~~~

WHAT BROUGHT YOU JOY AS A CHILD?

Think back to your experience as a child. How did you express your joy? Did you laugh uncontrollably? Dance around? Scream and shout? Pay close attention to how it made you feel to simply express your joy.

JUNE

~~~

You are the only person who is responsible for your joy.

10

〜〜〜

Black joy is an act of defiance. I am here to be an archer of joy and happiness, and I will use my weapon.

—YVONNE ORJI

11
JUNE

~

YOU DESERVE JOY

We block ourselves from experiencing joy and happiness when we don't believe we truly deserve it. Take a moment to think about your relationship with joy. If you struggle with letting yourself be joyful, remember that the more you remain present, the easier it will become to fill your life with joy.

12
JUNE

~

Joy exists wherever you can imagine it. Find joy in the very simple things in life.

13
JUNE

AFFIRMATION

I deserve pleasure for the sake of pleasure.

14
JUNE

BE PRESENT WITH YOUR JOY

The next time you experience joy, allow yourself to be fully immersed in the moment. Don't think about the past or the future—simply focus on being present and giving yourself the pleasure you deserve.

15
JUNE

Allow yourself to FULLJOY: fully enjoy life,
rather than just enjoy it.

16
JUNE

FIND SOMETHING NEW

Although we have an idea of how we experience and understand
our own happiness, there are so many ways we can explore joy. Try
doing something new, even if it's small. You may be surprised at the
fulfillment it brings you.

17
JUNE

Surrounding yourself with joy is just as important as allowing yourself to experience it.

18
JUNE

BE A JOYFUL PERSON

Only once we embrace our true, authentic selves can we unlock the joy that comes from simply being. Think about the things you do and analyze the patterns in which you do them. Then write down five things you like about the way you do things and how you can explore them. For example, if you like the way you cook, put more intention and joy into the foods you make for yourself.

19
JUNE

I'm starting to redefine where my joy comes from, and for me it is rooted in family, friends, and memories.

—DANIELLE BROOKS

20
JUNE

BE CONSISTENT WITH YOUR GRATITUDE

This evening, take some time to list everything that brought you joy throughout your day. In reviewing your list, remember to be grateful for every moment of enjoyment.

21
JUNE

When we express our own joy, we remind others to experience joy.

22
JUNE

~

SPARK SOME JOY!

When was the last time you had a positive, fulfilling conversation? Carve out some time today to indulge in conversations that remind you of how beautiful this life can be. Have a chat with anyone who sparks some joy in your life!

23
JUNE

~

Stop wedding your happiness to accomplishments.
Be happy now—right where you are.

24
JUNE

~~~

JOY ISN'T ALWAYS ACTIVE

Although joy can be active, you can still experience it by relaxing, resting, and taking it easy. Make sure you take some time each day to rest in an enjoyable way. It could mean having a nap that reenergizes you, soaking in a hot bath, or taking a break from your to-do list. Whatever it is, don't forget to enjoy giving your body what it needs.

25
JUNE

Rejoice in building and living a life that is filled with joy.

26
JUNE

AFFIRMATION

I embrace my divine feminine energy through love, laughter, and joy.

27

JUNE

~~~

STOP PUNISHING YOURSELF

When we constantly punish ourselves for our mistakes, we stop ourselves from experiencing joy. Many of us fall into the trap of punishing ourselves over and over for the same mistake, or for failing at something. Reflect on the times you may have stopped yourself from experiencing joy because you didn't think you deserved it.

28

JUNE

~~~

Make joy a priority.

29
JUNE

Celia Cruz, or the "Queen of Salsa," was an Afro-Cuban singer and entertainer. Cruz was a major contributor to the popularization of the genre in the United States. She shared her culture unapologetically and it earned her countless international accolades. She was known for her natural zest and sense of humor. Think about the many ways you can express joy and how it can spark happiness in the lives of others.

30
JUNE

I realized that I don't have to be perfect. All I have to do is show up and enjoy the messy, imperfect, and beautiful journey of my life.

—KERRY WASHINGTON

JULY
SISTERHOOD

JULY

WHAT IS SISTERHOOD TO YOU?

Today, spend some time thinking about your friendships with other Black women. What do you like about your friendships? What don't you like about them? What would you change about them? Think deeply about what you need in a friendship, as well as what you can give. It's important to be aware of the type of friendships you want and need so you can begin building fulfilling relationships.

2

JULY

To experience true sisterhood, we must unlearn the harmful stereotypes we are fed and subconsciously associate with ourselves.

3

JULY

AFFIRMATION

I reflect and exude the same beauty I see in my sisters.

4

JULY

~~~

WHAT IS YOUR SHARED EXPERIENCE?

Reflect on your experience in society as a Black woman. You have likely encountered scenarios that unfolded a specific way as a result of the intersection between your race and sex. Realize this experience is unique to Black women, and the only people who can understand your experience entirely are Black women.

5

JULY

~~~

Your sisters are those who understand you, validate your experience, and embrace you as you are.

Historically, the feminist movement blatantly ignored the Black woman's experience, rather than fighting for *all* women's rights. **The Black Feminist Movement** (which sparked intersectional feminism) filled this gap, creating an agenda that acknowledged our experience and fought for the liberation of Black women. Scholars like Kimberlé Williams Crenshaw, bell hooks, Patricia Hill Collins, and Angela Davis have made substantial contributions to the theories and beliefs that underlie the Black Feminist Movement. Take some time to think about the exclusivity of the feminist movement, and the premise of Black Feminism.

7
JULY

MISOGYNY VERSUS MISOGYNOIR

The word *misogyny* refers to prejudice and mistreatment of women. *Misogynoir* is defined as hate, dislike, and prejudice specifically against Black women. Reflect on the distinction between these terms.

8
JULY

Remember that your experience as a Black woman is just yours. Although there may be similarities in our experiences, we all have an experience that is unique to us.

9

JULY

~~~

WHERE WAS THE LAST PLACE YOU FELT SAFE?

As Black women, we often seek "safe spaces" or inclusive areas where we can be welcomed for and unapologetic about who we are. Think about the last space you entered where you felt fully embraced.

10

JULY

~~~

Sisterhood exists beyond boundaries, beyond country, beyond age, and beyond time.

11

JULY

~

WHICH BLACK WOMEN INSPIRE YOU?

Think about the Black women who inspire you. These could be your mother, auntie, best friend, etc. Think about how you can ignite a true sisterhood in these relationships. If you feel you already have, think about how you can deepen the relationship.

12

JULY

~

The "strong black woman" trope, although historically celebrated, can be extremely harmful for Black women to believe and chase.

13
JULY

CALL ON YOUR SISTERS

When things get difficult, we often turn inward and block ourselves from relying on our sisters in a time of need. Think about the last time you went through a challenging time. Who was there to support you, even in the smallest ways? Did you allow them to be there for you? The next time you face a rough patch, let yourself rely on your sisters for help. You don't have to do it all alone!

14
JULY

Relying on your sisters for help when you need it does not make you weak.

15
JULY

WHAT DID YOU LEARN ABOUT SISTERHOOD?

Take some time to reflect on what you were taught about sisterhood. Was it something positive that you were introduced to or were you taught to avoid it? Think about what it means to build friendship and connection into a sisterhood.

16

JULY

~~~

To reunite with Black women is to reunite with yourself.

17

JULY

~~~

AFFIRMATION

I am supported, loved, and protected by my sisters.

18
JULY

~~~

HOW CAN YOU HELP?

Think about the last time you were there for a friend in a time of need.
Were you emotionally present for them? Did you surprise them or
maybe run a few errands for them? To build these genuine friendships,
we must be willing to help our sisters, the same way we ourselves
sometimes need help.

19
JULY

~~~

The interactions Black women have with one another are
therapeutic in so many ways.

20

~~~~~

KNOW YOUR BOUNDARIES

For a friendship to flourish into a sisterhood, it's important to remember we all have different boundaries and needs. Being a good friend doesn't necessarily mean you and your friend(s) talk or see each other every day. The bulk of the friendship really lies in mutual respect and love. Make a list of healthy boundaries you want to maintain in your friendships. If you feel more comfortable without physical touch, you may write down that you have a physical boundary. If you have a specific schedule, you could write down that you have a time boundary.

21
JULY

~~~~~

Platonic love is just as important as romantic love.

22
JULY

~

WHEN SHE WINS, YOU WIN

When a Black woman wins, we all win. There is a pride that follows us, knowing and seeing excellence among us. Reflect on a time you were proud to see another Black woman win or succeed at something.

23
JULY

~

I am a product of every other Black woman before me who has done or said anything worthwhile. Recognizing that I am part of history is what allows me to soar.

—OPRAH WINFREY

24
JULY

CONNECT WITH YOUR SISTERS

Today, spend some time connecting with your sisters. If you have the capacity, engage in a conversation where you can all be open, real, and genuine. It's important to get into the habit of checking in with your friends, even if you can't be there for one another all day, every day.

25
JULY

Grandmothers, mothers, sisters, aunties, cousins—these are our first introductions to true Black sisterhood.

26
JULY

Olive Morris was born in Jamaica and became a Britain-based Black feminist, activist, and member of the Black Panther Party. While in England, Morris became a founding member of groups like the Brixton Black Women's Group and the Organisation of Women of African and Asian Descent (OWAAD). Reflect on sisterhood and the existence of Black Feminism and sisterhood beyond borders.

27
JULY

~

WHAT DOES *SISTERHOOD* MEAN TO YOU?

Spend some time thinking about what the word *sisterhood* represents
to you and its place in your life.

28
JULY

~

To experience true sisterhood, you must first become the
sister you needed in hardship.

29
JULY

~~~

Gain strength by drawing on the love your sisters
show you. Remember to inhabit the love you feel
in sisterhood.

30
JULY
~~

I wouldn't be here without all of the Black women around me. Put us together, and we can do anything.

—MISTY COPELAND

31
JULY
~~

There is safety in genuine sisterhood.

AUGUST
REST

1

AUGUST

~~~

WHAT DOES REST FEEL LIKE?

Take some time to think about the different ways you've felt rested. These experiences may include sitting after spending a long time on your feet, taking a mental rest from a big project, or turning off your phone notifications for a sensory rest. Make a list of all these instances and review the different types of rest that come up.

2

AUGUST

~~~

Too often, we treat rest as a reward,
rather than a necessity.

3
AUGUST

~

AFFIRMATION

I am in touch with and aware of my body,
and the rest I need to function.

AUGUST

~

WHEN WAS THE LAST TIME YOU TRULY RESTED?

Reflect on the last time you woke up feeling well-rested. What did
you do before your rest? How long did you sleep? What did it feel like
to wake up? If you can't remember the last time you slept well, try to
identify what may be blocking you from getting the rest you need.

5
AUGUST

Hard work must be balanced with rest for you to grow and reach lasting success.

6
AUGUST

A LACK OF REST IS COSTLY

Think about how you feel when you aren't well-rested. Are you grumpy? Frustrated? Do you feel like you're on autopilot all the time? It's important to know the signs of when we haven't been taking the necessary time to rest and rejuvenate ourselves.

7

AUGUST

~~~

Working hard toward being your best self isn't possible
without rest.

8

AUGUST

~~~

PAY ATTENTION TO THE PATTERNS

Think about your resting patterns. Do you usually feel mentally or
physically exhausted after a day of work or school? Do you find it takes
you a long time to fall asleep at night? Paying close attention to these
patterns may help reveal helpful cues about how we experience rest
deprivation. If we can pinpoint these symptoms, we can work toward
giving ourselves the rest we need.

9

AUGUST

Sleep is just one way to rest. But for many of us, unfortunately, it is the only rest we get.

10

AUGUST

SLEEP IS NOT ALL YOU NEED

Take some time to explore a different type of rest, aside from sleep (passive rest). Other types of rest include mental rest (meditation, short breaks from work), physical rest (yoga, breathing exercises), sensory rest (screen breaks, turning off all electronics/notifications), digestive rest (fasting, boundaries around eating late at night), and social rest (texting/talking breaks). Rest looks different to everybody, but the idea is to find what works for us. Make a list of the different types of rest you've identified, and don't be afraid to try something new!

11
AUGUST

~~~

You are allowed to prioritize your rest, even if it means
saying no to people.

12
AUGUST

~~~

Tricia Hersey-Patrick is a performance artist, poet, and activist. As
the founder of the Nap Ministry, Hersey-Patrick advocates for rest
as an act of resistance for Black people, particularly Black women.
Through her community healing work, Hersey-Patrick has facilitated
educational programs, experiences, and practices to help heal the
Black community through rest. Consider the current pace of your life,
and the type of pace you wish to have going forward.

13

AUGUST

UNPLUG YOURSELF

In our digitally driven world, it can be difficult to get rest with the constant distraction of notifications, sounds, pictures, and videos on our devices. Today, try to give yourself a rest from all technology. Scroll less, text less, and give yourself a chance to live outside your digital life.

14

AUGUST

When I'm tired, I rest. I say, "I can't be a superwoman today."

—JADA PINKETT SMITH

AUGUST

~~~

GIVE YOURSELF PERMISSION TO REST

Often we don't allow ourselves to ease into a state of rest. Many of us (including me!) are guilty of finishing up some emails and then heading straight to bed right afterward. When we throw ourselves into sleep, it makes it more difficult for our body to rest properly. Today, spend some time making a list of things you can do to help yourself prepare for bed by shifting into "rest mode."

16
AUGUST

Allowing yourself to rest is allowing yourself to live.

17
AUGUST

CREATE A MORNING ROUTINE

Similar to jolting ourselves into sleep mode after working, many of us wake up in the mornings and throw ourselves into work. We push our body to perform so much without giving it an opportunity to truly wake up. Tonight, spend some time planning a morning routine for tomorrow. Think about the ways you can ease out of rest mode. It could be through quieting your thoughts for a mental rest, or social rest by limiting the amount you are talking in the mornings. If you're having trouble coming up with a plan, think about what an ideal, calm morning looks like for you.

18
AUGUST

~~~~

There is something so revolutionary about seeing a Black woman chilling.

—EBONYJANICE MOORE

19

~~~~

WHAT DO YOU THINK OF REST?

As Black people, we have learned that sitting still and doing "nothing" is a sign of laziness. It stems from the deep, harmful beliefs our people were fed during slavery. Being found not working led to excruciating punishment and even death. Reflect on your perspective of rest. If you see it as negative, question this idea and try your best to look at rest as a necessity for your well-being.

20
AUGUST

~~~

Society teaches us that constantly being busy and having a full schedule add value to who we are. Although it is important to work hard for the things we want to achieve, all we can ask of ourselves is our best.

21
AUGUST

~~~

CREATE A NIGHTTIME ROUTINE

It may be difficult to incorporate rest into a busy life, especially if the concept of rest is brand-new. Creating a consistent routine for rest can support these changes in our life. Tonight, try working on creating a nightly routine. What can you do each night to prepare yourself for sleep? It could be turning off all electronics by 8 p.m. or doing some stretching before heading to bed. Think back to the activities you tried on August 10 and reflect on the list you made that day.

22
AUGUST

~~~

Rest is a healing space.

23
AUGUST

~~~

STOP RESISTING REST

We've all resisted sleep at one point or another. Maybe it was to complete an important task or to finish a new binge-worthy show. But when have you resisted the things that keep you from resting? Of course, there are times we may be too busy to get the rest we need, because that's life. But this week, try your best to minimize anything preventing you from sleeping. Do you have to finish that email or can it wait until tomorrow?

24
AUGUST

～

Listen to your body and pay close attention to the signs it
communicates to you. A lack of rest shows itself in
and on the body in many ways.

25
AUGUST

～

AFFIRMATION

My worth is not determined by my productivity.

26

PRACTICE RESTING

In a typical week, most of us will look to the weekend as a designated time of rest. This habit often puts pressure on us, and weekends end up being packed with the things we don't finish during the week. Rather than look at a day of the week as a time to rest, incorporate at least one type of rest in your schedule every day. Doing so will support you in building a consistent practice of rest.

27
AUGUST

Challenge the idea that you must work yourself
to the bone to be successful.

28
AUGUST

AFFIRMATION

I am deserving of full, deep, rejuvenating rest.

29
AUGUST

~~~

Khadija Nelson is the founder of the LIV Collective, a Toronto-based healing space for Black women and Women of Color. The LIV Collective is made up of Black yoga teachers, writers, and therapists who aim to support Black women and Women of Color on their healing journeys. In many resting and healing spaces, Black women do not feel welcomed, and many have racist experiences. Think about collective rest and what that may look and feel like for Black women.

30
AUGUST

~

Action also requires rest. Give yourself permission to do both.

—ALEXANDRA ELLE

31
AUGUST

~

Robbing yourself of rest aligns with the colonialist agenda created to dehumanize Black people.

SEPTEMBER
RESET

1

SEPTEMBER

MAXIMIZE YOUR RESET

Take some time to focus on the future. What do you want to accomplish? What must you do now in your reset to prepare to achieve your goals?

2

SEPTEMBER

Familiarize yourself with the act of repeatedly resetting.

3
SEPTEMBER

~~~

RESET YOUR BODY

Today, challenge yourself to reset your body. If you have been feeling any aches or pains, think about how you can reset your body, either through moving or resting it.

4
SEPTEMBER

~~~

Taking the time to reset is a vital part of the journey toward achieving any goal.

5

SEPTEMBER

REMEMBER YOUR GOALS

Remember the list of goals you created at the beginning of this year? Spend some time revisiting and reviewing this list. So many things have happened from January up to this point. In reviewing your list, ask yourself: Is this still a goal? Is it a priority? How can I set myself up for success right now? What hasn't been working on this journey to achieving my goals? Taking the time to reflect during a time of reset allows you to refocus on what really matters.

6

SEPTEMBER

Our priorities, wants, and needs change as we grow. When we step back to reset, we grant ourselves the opportunity to better provide ourselves with those very wants and needs.

7

SEPTEMBER

~~~

Jully Black is a Canadian-Caribbean singer/songwriter, actress, and producer. In her TEDx Talk "How to Rewrite Your Life," she brought attention to the many different versions of ourselves, explaining that, in order to grow in this life, we must continue to "let go." Her speech reminds us that each moment we have is a new opportunity to choose differently for ourselves. Knowing this, what might you reset and approach differently in your life? What can you do right now to reset and make a choice that brings you one step closer to your goals?

8

SEPTEMBER

~

REFLECTION

Reflect on how far you've come on your journey. Remind yourself that although this is a lifelong path, your growth deserves to be acknowledged and celebrated. It is an important practice because each time you reset, you operate from a place of higher knowledge. Now that you know better and have done better, how can you challenge yourself to be better?

9

SEPTEMBER

~

It's never too late to restart.

10
SEPTEMBER

~~~

RESET YOUR SURROUNDINGS

Spend some time today decluttering your space. As we continue through life, we accumulate so many things that have the potential to clutter more than just our space. Be intentional and get rid of things that weigh you down.

11
SEPTEMBER

~~~

Stop being afraid of failing. Failing is just one indicator that we need to reset, adjust, and approach the situation another way.

SEPTEMBER

Do the best you can until you know better.
Then when you know better, do better.

—DR. MAYA ANGELOU

SEPTEMBER

MAKE YOUR MIND A SAFE SPACE

Spend some time sifting through your mind today. What have your thoughts been like? How have you been talking to yourself in your mind? Quite often, we fall back into hurtful ways of treating ourselves. If you've noticed a harsher approach to how you have been treating yourself lately, try revisiting March: Self-Care. It may help you reignite some forgiveness and compassion for yourself.

14
SEPTEMBER

We avoid burning out when we allow ourselves time to
step back, reset, and reapproach life.
Resetting allows for refocus.

15
SEPTEMBER

RESET YOUR RELATIONSHIPS

Take some time today to review your group of friends and loved ones. As we continue to evolve, it's important to keep in line with our positive journey. Sometimes the people surrounding us don't align with this path. Evaluate who has supported you throughout this journey and if you come across a relationship that is no longer serving you positively, consider reaching out to that person to express your feelings. If that doesn't help, it's worth considering ending the relationship.

16
SEPTEMBER

We have the constant choice to reset in life.
We live a cycle of starting, enduring, and restarting
with each passing day.

17
SEPTEMBER

~~~

FOCUS ON NOURISHING YOUR BODY

Feeding ourselves can be particularly challenging, especially when we fall into patterns of eating food that isn't nutritious or beneficial to our bodies. Today, without judgment, review your dietary habits from this year so far. If you aren't happy with the foods you have been consuming, consider resetting your diet to include healthier, more nutritious, and rejuvenating foods.

18
SEPTEMBER

~~~

Resetting can be a process of holding yourself accountable for your goals.

19
SEPTEMBER

You can fall, but you can rise also.

—ANGÉLIQUE KIDJO

20
SEPTEMBER

AGE IS ONLY A NUMBER

Society tells us that once we have reached a certain age, we become "too old" to accomplish our goals or even change them. We are bombarded with pressure to achieve success before getting "too old." Spend some time challenging this idea and consider the growth that comes with achieving our goals later in life. Remember there is no age attached to resetting and starting over.

21
SEPTEMBER

Following a specific morning or nighttime routine supports a consistent reset to begin and end your day.

22
SEPTEMBER

FAIL FORWARD

We are constantly sold the idea that failure is a negative experience—it's embarrassing, it's impossible to come back from, and, worst of all, it means we can't try again. Think about things you once failed at. Did you try again afterward? If so, did you do any better the second time around? If not, what stopped you from trying again? It's important to remember that failing is just a step. We can always reset, try again, and achieve more than we ever could have imagined.

23
SEPTEMBER

When we consistently reset different areas of our life, we prepare to leap ahead from a solid foundation.

24
SEPTEMBER

AFFIRMATION

I choose to invest in my overall well-being each day.

25

SEPTEMBER

REBOOT

In this age of technology, we often have to restart our devices when they are updated or not working properly. Although they are machines, they still need to be reset every once in a while in order to function. Think about what this may mean for humans. Given that we aren't machines, what do you think the benefits of resetting look like for us?

26
SEPTEMBER

~~~

Before stepping into her career in the film industry at the age of 32, **Ava DuVernay** began her career in public relations. She likely faced many comments and doubts around her choice to reset her career at her age. Now an award-winning director, DuVernay has become an icon in the Black community for her ability to tell stories through film. Think about what her life may have looked like today if she had decided to listen to the doubts and negativity around resetting and restarting.

27

REFRESH AND PREP

Resetting allows us to ignite our creativity to reapproach life in a fulfilling way. Carve out some time today to evaluate and accept where you are on this journey. Then get creative about the next three months of the year. How can you do things differently? How can you be kinder to yourself? How can you use this tool of resetting to benefit you on this journey? Don't forget to celebrate all the work you've done so far.

28
SEPTEMBER

In this journey, you will experience many resets.
Get familiar with them and learn how you can reach
your full potential by strategically resetting.

29
SEPTEMBER

When we reset the body, we give it the rejuvenation it
needs to carry us forward.

30
SEPTEMBER

If you're on a path that's not the one that you want to be on, you can also pivot, and you can also move, and age doesn't make a difference, [neither do] race, gender. It's about putting one step in front of another, about forward movement to where you wanna be.

—AVA DUVERNAY

OCTOBER
FACING YOUR FEARS

OCTOBER

WHAT ARE YOU AFRAID OF?

When we think about our fears, we often see them as things to avoid and run away from. Today, spend some time reflecting on the things that scare you. Make a list of all the things you are afraid of.

OCTOBER

Do not fear change—embrace it.

3
OCTOBER

~

FIND OUT YOUR CORE FEARS

Using the list of fears you made on October 1, categorize them based on your deeper core fears. For example, if you listed "performing in front of an audience" as a fear, your core fear could be that you're afraid of looking silly to other people. If you listed that you're afraid to try new things, the core fear is likely that you are afraid of failure. Do this exercise for each fear on your list. Pay close attention to any patterns you see.

4
OCTOBER

~

Face your fears with the people closest to you.

5
OCTOBER

It's only when you risk failure that you discover things. When you play it safe, you're not expressing the utmost of your human experience.

—LUPITA NYONG'O

6
OCTOBER

AFFIRMATION

Each "failure" I experience is packed with invaluable lessons. I learn and flourish with each failure.

7

OCTOBER

~~~

WHAT'S STOPPING YOU?

Spend some time reflecting on your list of goals today. Sometimes, even when we set out to accomplish our goals, we subconsciously stop ourselves from working toward them because of fear. Take your time reviewing the list and identify what you may be stopping yourself from doing. The first step is recognizing your fear.

8

OCTOBER

~~~

When you stop trying new things, you stop yourself from truly experiencing life.

9

OCTOBER

~~~

Luvvie Ajayi Jones is a Nigerian-born best-selling author, digital strategist, and keynote speaker. After being approached to present a TED Talk and declining twice, Jones realized her own fears were keeping her from taking advantage of the amazing opportunities around her. Take a moment to reflect on the decisions you've made based on fear. If Jones had said no to the TED Talk opportunity for a third time, how do you think she would have felt afterward?

10

OCTOBER

~~~

FREAK YOURSELF OUT

Do something that scares you today. It could be taking a different route home from work or school, trying a new activity, or initiating a conversation. No matter what it is, focus on the feeling of accomplishment you'll have after facing just one small fear.

11
OCTOBER

It's okay to be scared.

12
OCTOBER

SHIFT YOUR MIND

We can think of thousands of ways for things to go wrong. Today, challenge that pattern. Instead of worrying about all the ways things could end badly, spend time dreaming about how amazingly well things could go instead.

13
OCTOBER

Do not allow your fears to control your every step in life.

14
OCTOBER

EXPLORE YOUR FEAR

Fear is a natural emotion we all need to experience. Each time you feel afraid, take a couple of minutes to reflect. Ask yourself: "What am I afraid of, and why am I afraid of it?" You may discover it's not a fear worth having at all.

15
OCTOBER

You will fail time and time again before you reach success. Fearing failure is fearing success.

16
OCTOBER

AFFIRMATION

I am not my failures.

17
OCTOBER

~~~

GET BACK ON THE HORSE

When we fall off the horse, we fear getting back on and having the same thing happen again. Remember that a story of success is one that includes many failures. With each failure comes an important lesson to move you further ahead before the next attempt. Spend some time reflecting on the last thing you failed at doing. What can you take away from this failure that will help you next time?

18
OCTOBER

~~~

When we challenge and overcome our fears,
we allow ourselves to grow and become a stronger,
better version of ourselves.

SIT WITH YOUR FEAR

Any moment you feel fear today, spend a moment sitting with it. A big part of facing and overcoming our fears is understanding where they come from and what triggers them. To do so, we must sit with our fears and question them. If you're struggling with this, try asking yourself these questions: When was the last time I experienced this same fear? What am I afraid will happen? Is this fear deep-rooted or just passing?

20
OCTOBER

~~~

The goal is not to eliminate fear, but to challenge
it as much as we can.

21
OCTOBER

~~~

In 1946, Canadian civil rights activist **Viola Desmond** refused to leave
the Whites-only section of Rosedale Theatre, a segregated theater
in New Glasgow, Nova Scotia. When she attempted to purchase a
floor seat, she was denied and given a balcony seat, reserved for
non-Whites. When she attempted to exchange the ticket for a floor
seat and pay the difference, she was denied once again. Desmond
then chose to sit in a floor seat and watch the movie. Police were
called and Desmond was dragged out of the theater and arrested.
Desmond's bravery gained her much attention, including her photo on
the $10 Canadian banknote. Take some time to reflect on Desmond's
bravery, and how it impacted Black Canadians.

IMAGINE A FEARLESS LIFE

Imagine what your life would be like if you didn't let fear hold you back. What would you do? What would you try? Who would you be? What could you learn and accomplish? Think big here!

I think the fear will always be there, but what's important is that I go forward anyway.

—LUVVIE AJAYI JONES

24
OCTOBER

A higher version of you lies on the other side of fear.

25
OCTOBER

THERE IS STRENGTH IN NUMBERS

You don't have to face your fears alone! Remember to allow yourself to ask for help when you need it. There is strength in numbers. The next time you feel afraid, reach out to a close friend or family member. Chances are, they'll know just what to say simply because they love and support you.

26
OCTOBER

~~~

A fear-based mind is a limited one.

27
OCTOBER

~~~

Others may try to instill fear in you.
Remember that if you believe in and trust yourself,
you can accomplish anything.

28

SHARE YOUR JOURNEY CAREFULLY

People will likely project their own fears onto you, especially if you are doing something new or unfamiliar to them. If it happens and you find it's discouraging you from facing your fears, try setting some healthy boundaries with them. It may mean keeping information about facing your fears to yourself, or speaking to them less frequently, especially if their criticism comes up in conversation.

29

OCTOBER

~~

FOCUS ON THE WAR, NOT THE BATTLE

Facing your fears means accepting what you're afraid of and still making the active choice to face it head-on. It doesn't always mean that we are successful in facing our fears every time. Today, remind yourself that facing your fears is a nonlinear process.

30

OCTOBER

~~

If we stay within the confines of our safe zones, we limit our own growth and ability to expand beyond our wildest dreams.

31
OCTOBER

AFFIRMATION

I accept that fear is part of my journey
and I refuse to let it stop me.

NOVEMBER
GRATITUDE

1
NOVEMBER

REFLECT ON YOUR CHILDHOOD

As children, we are often grateful for the simplest things. Spend some time reflecting on your childhood. What do you remember being grateful for? What simple things brought you the most joy?

2
NOVEMBER

Don't turn your gratitude into complacency. Being grateful for small things does not mean you cannot work toward achieving more.

3

NOVEMBER

~~~

GRATITUDE ATTRACTS ABUNDANCE

When we focus on being grateful, we invite more positivity and abundance into our lives. From today forward, spend time each day creating a list of things you are grateful for. Write down at least 10 different things, experiences, and people you are grateful for each morning, and pay close attention to the shifts you may begin to experience.

4

NOVEMBER

~~~

The best thing about gratitude is it never fails. You can always find something to be grateful for.

5

NOVEMBER

〜

WHAT IS GRATITUDE TO YOU?

Reflect on what gratitude means to you. Think about how you feel when you are grateful and how it impacts your mood, thoughts, and beliefs.

6

NOVEMBER

〜

Practicing gratitude is just that—a practice. The more you do it, the better you get at it and the easier it becomes.

We think we have to do something to be grateful or something has to be done in order for us to be grateful, when gratitude is a state of being.

—IYANLA VANZANT

8

NOVEMBER

HOW DO YOU SHOW YOUR GRATITUDE?

Reflect on how you have shown others that you are thankful for them. It may be through DIY gifts, a phone call, a sweet message, or a surprise! Reflect on how it feels to show others you are grateful to have them in your life. Also think about how it may make them feel to know you appreciate them.

9

NOVEMBER

Be grateful for your struggles. Without them, you wouldn't be who you are today. You're smarter, you're stronger, and you continue to evolve with each day.

10
NOVEMBER
~~~

British actress **Kelechi Okafor** shared her opinions around gratitude after learning that Tiffany Haddish, a famous comedian and actress, was asked to host the Grammys without compensation. Okafor noted that she is "grateful to the divine . . . to God for the opportunities that come to [her] and . . . grateful to [her] ancestors [who] continue to ride with [her] every step of the way." However, she refused to extend her gratitude to "an institution," explaining that "[They] should be grateful to [her] for the very divinity sitting at [their] table." Take a moment to reflect on the balance between gratitude and fighting for what you deserve and, sometimes, asking for more than is offered.

11

NOVEMBER

~~~

BEING GRATEFUL IS BEING PRESENT

When we are grateful for all we have, we allow ourselves to live in the present and experience life to the fullest. In each moment you find yourself grateful for something, allow yourself to expand that gratitude. You just might experience a few bursts of positive energy!

12

NOVEMBER

~~~

The more gratitude you show, the more positivity you invite into your life.

13
NOVEMBER

~~~

GRATITUDE DOES NOT ELIMINATE SADNESS

Being grateful doesn't mean you won't encounter sadness in life. Remember all emotions remind us that we are alive—that we are human. The next time you find yourself upset or frustrated, don't run away from this feeling. Instead, acknowledge it and allow yourself to *feel* your feelings. Rather than getting stuck in your sadness, use gratitude as a tool to lift yourself up.

14
NOVEMBER

~~~

When you're thankful and focus on what you already have in life, you don't obsess and become disappointed over what you don't have.

15
NOVEMBER

〜

CHALLENGES EQUAL GROWTH

Spend some time reflecting on the last time you encountered a challenge that helped you grow. Although it was difficult, you conquered it and evolved into a stronger, higher version of yourself.

16
NOVEMBER

〜

Being grateful isn't always easy. You must find ways to give thanks every day to experience the true gifts that gratitude brings.

17

NOVEMBER

The ability to be grateful is something to be grateful for.

—KAILEI CARR

18

NOVEMBER

〜

BE GRATEFUL FOR YOUR JOURNEY

Using the list of goals you created in January, spend some time being grateful for your journey toward achieving these goals. Be grateful for each goal as though you have already accomplished it. It is one way to manifest your deepest dreams while appreciating where you are in life.

19

NOVEMBER

〜

There is nothing too small to be grateful for. The more we pay attention to the little things, the more we fill our lives with gratitude and abundance.

20
NOVEMBER

~

BACK TO BASICS

We often forget to be thankful when our basic needs are met. Today, be grateful for waking up this morning, the food you eat multiple times throughout the day, the pillow you lay your head on at night, and the roof over your head. It's important to acknowledge and honor these blessings. Many people are happier with less than what you have.

21
NOVEMBER

~

There is no "need" in gratitude.

22
NOVEMBER

~

AFFIRMATION

I am grateful for a life that is filled with love, happiness, and abundance.

23
NOVEMBER

~

Gratitude is the key to unlocking a life filled with happiness.

24
NOVEMBER

SHOW YOURSELF SOME GRATITUDE

Spend moments throughout the day being grateful for you. Through all the challenges, the good times and the bad, you have been there for yourself. Celebrate this and rejoice in gratitude for being the person you are! You have gotten yourself this far.

25

~~~

LIMIT THE NEGATIVITY

It's common for us to complain daily about the things we don't like. We spend time upset about traffic, work schedules, and responsibilities. Soon enough, our complaints trump our gratitude and we become overpowered by them. Be cognizant of the things you complain about today that you can change as opposed to the things you can't. Remember that the more energy you put toward complaining, the more negativity you attract to your life.

26

~~~

DIFFERENT DOESN'T MEAN *WORSE*

When things don't go as we planned, we often get angry and upset. But when we forget to be grateful for things, even when they aren't exactly how we want them, we forget to see the blessing. Today, spend some time thinking about something going differently and ending up even better in the long run.

27

~~~

Writing down the things you are grateful for is like
making a list of what you want more of in your life.
Write them, read them, feel them, and you will
continue to experience them.

28
NOVEMBER

~~~

Shonda Rhimes is a successful American television producer, screenwriter, and author. As the brain behind some of prime time's most awarded shows, Rhimes still prioritizes taking time to be grateful each day. When she sat down to begin writing her first gratitude list, she struggled for more than an hour before being able to write down just one thing to be grateful for. Eventually, it got easier and easier as she continued to write. Think about the concept of gratitude versus success and how gratitude plays a role in living a full, happy life.

29
NOVEMBER

~~~

AFFIRMATION

All I have is all I need.

30

NOVEMBER

Thank you is the best prayer that anyone could say. I say that one a lot. *Thank you* expresses extreme gratitude, humility, [and] understanding.

—ALICE WALKER

DECEMBER
BOUNDARIES

1

DECEMBER

~~~

WHAT ARE YOUR BOUNDARIES?

Boundaries can be particularly challenging to put in place. Remember that boundaries aren't there to punish anyone, but to maintain healthy, happy relationships—both with self and with others. Dedicate some time to making a list of your own boundaries. They could be sticking to a budget, refusing to be spoken to in a disrespectful way, or choosing to rest instead of going out. Pay close attention to any patterns you notice.

2

DECEMBER

~~~

December is a time of rejoicing and spending time with loved ones. Don't forget to prioritize your own wellness and to fill up your well during the holiday season. Setting boundaries is necessary for a happy life.

3

DECEMBER

YOU ARE ALLOWED TO INDULGE

It's important to allow ourselves to indulge, especially during the holiday season. Try to balance your indulgence by exercising your boundaries with yourself. When we indulge in moderation, we learn to appreciate our indulgences far more.

4

DECEMBER

It's important to respect your own financial boundaries. This season, focus less on the cost of gifts, and more on your love and appreciation as gifts. The priceless gifts are usually the best.

5

DECEMBER

FLEXIBILITY IN YOUR BOUNDARIES

Although we set our boundaries, sometimes we may need to adjust them. Your boundaries should be flexible enough to accommodate some change. Create a list of nonnegotiable boundaries so you can reference what you are willing to be flexible on, and what you are not. When our boundaries are clear to us, it eases the process of communicating them to others.

6

DECEMBER

~~~

Kim Knight, a licensed mental health counselor and therapist, and the certified life coach behind K. Knight Counseling, says it is important to know your boundaries will not always be respected. Knight encourages her clients to prepare for this eventuality. She also advises us to truly evaluate our relationship with someone if they are not willing to respect our boundaries. Take a moment to think about the boundaries you've set and how they are being respected. If you realize some of your relationships are struggling because of boundary issues, think about why that may be and how this relationship contributes to your happiness.

7

DECEMBER

~~~

Your boundaries are not in place to punish others.

8

DECEMBER

~~~

WHEN YOU DON'T HONOR YOUR BOUNDARIES

Today, reflect on the last time you did not honor your own boundaries. Think deeply about how you felt and how it impacted your mood or your physical body. When we can understand instances of not honoring our own boundaries, we can learn to do a better job upholding our boundaries.

9

DECEMBER

~~~

"*No*" is a full sentence.

10
DECEMBER

BOUNDARIES ARE NECESSARY

There are many reasons we fail to set boundaries. Sometimes we aren't aware that a boundary is needed, or we may not think we deserve to have a boundary respected, or we fear hurting others in the process of setting them. Reflect on the times you haven't set a boundary and evaluate why you may have avoided doing so.

11
DECEMBER

AFFIRMATION

I honor my boundaries so I can show up as my best self.

12
DECEMBER

Practice honoring your boundaries every day.

13
DECEMBER

DON'T APOLOGIZE FOR YOUR BOUNDARIES

Sometimes when we set boundaries, others may feel hurt or upset. Remember you cannot control how others respond to your boundaries. If someone tells you they are upset with the boundaries you have set, remind them you set these boundaries to help you both maintain a healthy, fulfilling relationship. Do not apologize for your boundaries and do not allow this reaction to sway you from keeping your boundaries in place.

14

DECEMBER

~~~

You deserve to have your boundaries respected.

15

DECEMBER

~~~

PRACTICE SETTING BOUNDARIES

Remember that implementing boundaries takes practice. There are many different places you can practice implementing them, but practicing with yourself is ideal. Start by giving yourself small boundaries to follow. The more you practice, the better you'll get. By honoring your own boundaries, you teach others how to treat you.

~

I always encourage people to come back to your [body]. If you use your body as your source, it will determine where your [boundaries] need to be drawn. If you don't give yourself sleep, your body will crash.

—DR. AYANNA ABRAMS

17
DECEMBER

Understanding your wants and needs is necessary
for creating healthy boundaries.

18
DECEMBER

WHEN YOUR BOUNDARIES ARE VIOLATED

When your boundaries are violated, it's important to let the person
know your true feelings. If you find that your boundaries are
consistently being disrespected, approach the person with a firm and
calm tone. You could also set actionable boundaries. For example,
"If you continue to speak to me that way, I will not continue this
conversation." This practice makes your boundaries clear to the
individual in a respectful way.

19
DECEMBER

~

Boundaries are not selfish.

20
DECEMBER

~

BE GENTLE WITH YOURSELF

It takes much practice to understand, communicate, and live while honoring your boundaries. If you find yourself frustrated with the journey, remember you are human! Be patient with yourself and focus on making progress rather than achieving perfection.

21

DECEMBER

~~~

AFFIRMATION

I allow myself to prioritize my own well-being,
even if it means disappointing others.

22

DECEMBER

~~~

Communication is key in understanding and respecting
your own boundaries and the boundaries of others.

23
DECEMBER

~~~

SAY *NO* MORE

Black women can fall into the habit of saying yes to others, even when we don't want to. By continuously saying yes, we overfill our plates, drowning in commitments. Today, practice saying no to the things you don't want to do. Remember you don't need to explain yourself.

24
DECEMBER

~~~

Failure to honor your boundaries will leave you burned out, tired, frustrated, empty, and even ill.

25

~

RESPECT OTHERS' BOUNDARIES

Just as you set your own boundaries, your family, friends, coworkers, etc., may also choose to impose their own boundaries. If you find yourself getting upset with the boundaries someone else has set for your relationship, evaluate why you feel this way. You may even engage in a conversation with that person to understand how you can better respect their boundaries.

26
DECEMBER

~

Listen to your body and your emotions—they will show you where your boundaries should lie.

27
DECEMBER

~~~

PARENTS AND BOUNDARIES

As you grow older, it can be especially challenging to set boundaries with your parents. To your parents, the dynamic between you and them will always be parent-to-child, and that largely affects how they perceive the boundaries you set for yourself. You may constantly try to please your parents, even if doing so doesn't align with what makes you happy. If you have a difficult time setting boundaries with your parents, remember it's not your job to please them. You have a life of your own and—with patience and communication—your parents can learn to respect the boundaries you have placed on the relationship.

28
DECEMBER

〜〜

Everybody has different boundaries. What is a boundary for others may not be a boundary for you—and that is okay!

29
DECEMBER

〜〜

Black women are consistently told we need to project an image as a "strong Black woman." Although this perspective can be motivating, it can also be extremely dangerous and dehumanizing. **Dr. Ayanna Abrams,** a clinical psychologist, is cofounder of Not So Strong, a Black woman–led movement that seeks to broaden the view of Black women beyond the impenetrable "strong Black woman" trope. Dr. Abrams explains that believing this trope can get in the way of Black women living our lives. It pushes us to overfunction, creating much distress and depression in our lives. Spend some time reflecting on your relationship with being a "strong Black woman." Have you put your health and wellness on the back burner to meet this expectation?

30

DECEMBER

~~~

The hardest part about setting boundaries with people, no matter who they are, is not feeling confident in our authority to do so. As long as you realize that setting boundaries is necessary for healthy relationships, you will feel better defining and keeping them.

—TAMERA MOWRY-HOUSLEY

31
DECEMBER

~~~

AFFIRMATION

I encourage others to respect my boundaries
by respecting my own boundaries.

References

Abrams, Ayanna, Dr. Not So Strong. NotSoStrong.org/about.

"Black History Month in Britain: Great Women You Should Know about—BBC Newsround." BBC News, October 1, 2018. BBC.co.uk/newsround/41433196.

Beck, Koa. "20 Quotes from Powerful Women on Gratitude." HerMoney, March 5, 2019. HerMoney.com/connect/friends/gratitude-quotes.

Boyd, Kayla. "Parenting, Baby Names, Celebrities, and Royal News." CafeMom, January 29, 2021. CafeMom.com/entertainment/210615-50-quotes-from-black-women/217820-jada_pinkett_smith.

Carr, Kailei. "Episode 187: The Power of Gratitude [Beyond Black Women—Day 3]." KaileiCarr.com, September 2, 2020. KaileiCarr.com/episode-187-the-power-of-gratitude-beyond-black-women-day-3.

Crenshaw, Kimberli. "Mapping the Margins: Intersectionality, Identity Politics, and Violence against Women of Color." *Stanford Law Review* 43, no. 6 (1991): 1241–1299. DOI:10.2307/1229039.

Curry, Colleen. Broadcast. "Maya Angelou's Wisdom Distilled in 10 of Her Best Quotes." ABC News, May 28, 2014. ABCNews.go.com/Entertainment/maya-angelous-wisdom-distilled-10-best-quotes/story?id=23895284.

Farley, Rebecca. "A Reminder from DuVernay: You Can Pivot at Any Point in Life." Ava DuVernay Storm Reid Facebook Live Interview. VICE Media Group, March 18, 2018. Refinery29.com/en-us/2018/03/193002/ava-duvernay-storm-reid-facebook-live.

Ferro, Abel. "Biography: Celia Cruz." Celia Cruz—The Queen of Salsa. Versal Studio, June 5, 2017. CeliaCruz.com/biography.

Grant, Jasmine. "Ayanna Abrams Explains Why Boundaries Strengthen Our Relationships." *Essence*, August 20, 2020. Essence.com/lifestyle/health-wellness/dr-ayanna-abrams-boundaries-strengthen-relationships.

McLeod, Nia Simone. "Black Women Quotes on Self-Love, Life, and Success." Everyday Power, June 3, 2021. EverydayPower.com/black-women-quotes.

Mowry-Housley, Tamera. "How Setting Boundaries Will Improve Relationships." ColonyCreative, July 14, 2017. TameraMowry.com/real-talk-setting-boundaries-will-improve-relationships.